100 GREAT

GAMES

THE REMIX

100 GREAT GAMES
THE REMIX

compiled by
Jon Sutherland and Nigel Gross

Piccolo Books
A Piccolo Original

For Paula and Julie,
the only two people we would
never dare play games with!

First published 1990 by Pan Books Ltd,
Cavaye Place, London SW10 9PG

9 8 7 6 5 4 3 2 1

Text © Jon Sutherland and Nigel Gross 1990
Illustrations © George Ajayi 1990

The right of Jon Sutherland and Nigel Gross to be
identified as authors of this work has been asserted by
them in accordance with the Copyright Designs and
Patents Act 1988.

The following games are strictly the copyright of
Sutherland and Gross 1989: Aliens, Boxing, Cops-and-
Robbers Car Chase, Cycle Race, Five-A-Side Cricket,
Dungeon, Escape! Five-A-Side Football, Golf, Lost City,
The Mile, Road Race, Shark, Stock Exchange, Treasure
Vault.

ISBN 0 330 31448 3

Printed and bound in Great Britain by
Clays Ltd, St Ives plc

CONTENTS

6. Alternative Games

7. Activity Games

8. Pencil and Paper Games

9. All New Games

INTRODUCTION

All the games in *100 Great Games: The Remix* are laid
out in exactly the same way. They are very easy to follow
and you can see at a glance how many people can play,
what you need for each game, whether it will be easy
or tricky to play and how much luck is involved!

The 'Complexity Level', which tells you how simple a
game will be, is shown on the left-hand side at the
beginning of each one. There is a scale, running from 1
to 5 ('very easy' to 'tricky') like this:

★   ★   ★   ★   ★

1   2   3   4   5

(1 = very easy; 2 = quite easy; 3 = average; 4 =
challenging; 5 = tricky)

So a game which is quite easy to play would look like
this:

★   ★

1   2   3   4   5

The 'Skill Level' is shown on the right-hand side at the
beginning of each game and tells you how much a game
relies on luck, or whether skill is important. The scale
works in the same way as the 'Complexity Level',
ranging from 1 ('luck only') to 5 ('very skilful').

A game that needs a lot of skill would look like this:

★   ★   ★   ★

1   2   3   4   5

The number of people who can play each game and the items needed for it are shown underneath the Complexity and Skill Levels (*see* the icon list on p. 9).

A typical game looks like this:

Name

Complexity Level   Skill Level

'Number of players' icon   'What you need' icons

Drawing of the board or set-up (if relevant)

Short introduction

RULES

HINTS

ICONS

One-player game (solo)

Pencil

Two-player game

Dice

Three-player game

Playing cards

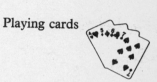

Multi-player game

Counters

Buy or make

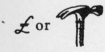

Sheets of paper

Chessboard

Card

Marbles

Balloons

Cushion

Dead matches

Blindfold

Old newspapers

Dominoes

Monopoly* houses

Music

**Fake money
(e.g. Monopoly* money)**

Scissors

Small object (e.g. thimble)

*'Monopoly' is a Trademark of Waddingtons Games Ltd.

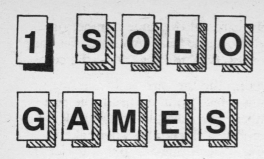

Clock Patience

★ ★   ★

1   2   3   4   5   1   2   3   4   5

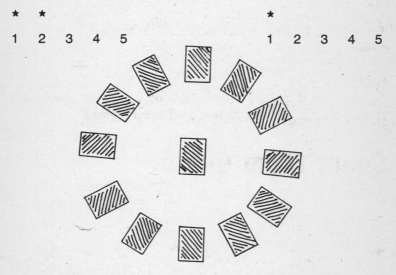

A very simple game, no skill required! You should not expect to win this very often though.

RULES

Deal out a full pack of cards as shown above, laying them out face down so that there are thirteen piles of four cards, twelve arranged like the numbers on the face of a clock, and one in the middle. The purpose of the game is to get all four cards of the same number on to the right pile around the clock-face. (Aces are one, jacks are eleven, queens are twelve and kings go in the centre.)

Start the game by taking the top card from the pile in the centre and placing it face up underneath the pile of the appropriate number. For example, if you pick up a four put it under the four o'clock pile. Then take the top card from the four o'clock pile and put it under the pile for that card's number. Continue playing until you are blocked, that is when you put the last card of a number on to a pile that does not have any face-down cards left.

To win, you must get all the cards on to their correct piles.

HINTS
You will need quite a bit of room on a table or the floor to play this game. Be patient and keep trying!

Count Them Out

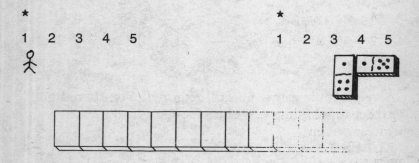

Another very simple game, needing no skill whatsoever!

RULES

Shuffle a full set of dominoes, then lay them out in a long line, face down. Turn all the dominoes over so that they are face up, keeping them in the line. Put your finger on the first domino in the line, then start counting from nought to twelve, moving your finger along to the next domino as you count. If you call out the same number as the total number on the domino (for example, a domino with 2 and 6 on it equals 8), then discard it. When you have counted up to twelve, start counting from nought again. When you get to the end of the line, start from the beginning again.

The idea of the game is to discard all the dominoes.

HINTS

None. Be prepared for a very long game. Count Them Out is ideal if you are bored and cannot be bothered with a game that is more difficult.

Domino Patience

★ ★   ★ ★ ★ ★

1 2 3 4 5   1 2 3 4 5

Quite a simple, but very skilful, game. Don't expect to win very often.

RULES

Shuffle the dominoes and lay them out end to end in a straight line, face down. Then turn them over so that they are face up. The idea of the game is to find matching pairs of dominoes next to each other. If two match, then you may discard them both. When you remove them, push the rest together to close up the gap.

To win you must discard all of the dominoes.

In the example below, you can discard the 3–6 and the 6–2. Note that only one half of each domino has to match in order to discard it. The same would be true of, say, the 4–1 and the 2–1.

HINTS
Take care in choosing which dominoes to discard. Often it is a good idea not to discard a particular pair if it will block your being able to remove other dominoes. Look ahead and try to figure out which is the best pair to discard before you do.

Klondike

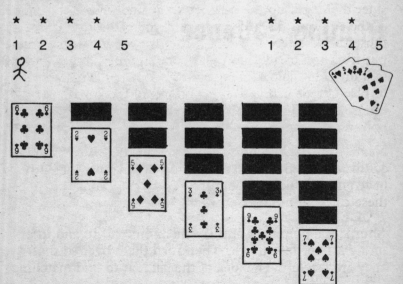

This is the best-known version of card patience. It is played throughout the world and is known by many different names, although the rules are virtually the same.

RULES

Deal a line of seven cards, with the first one face up and the others face down. Then deal out a line of six cards, putting them on top of the face-down cards in the first line (in other words, starting from the second card in the line). Again, the first card should be face up and the others face down. Then deal out five cards, in the same way, then four, three, two and one. The remainder of the pack should be placed to the side. You are now ready to play.

The idea of the game is to remove all the cards from the lines and from the remainder of the pack and to put them in order, from ace to king, in their suits.

If there is an ace face up, remove it and put it to the side, then turn up the card that was underneath it. Look at the columns of cards and see if you can move any of those that are face up. You can move a card so that you put it on top of another that is one number higher and of a different colour. You can only put red cards on top of black cards or black cards on top of red cards. For example, a red five can be put on top of a black six, but not on top of a red six.

Next, you should look to see if any of the face-up cards can be removed and placed on top of any aces that you have already taken out and put aside. You must put these cards in number order of the same suit.

You can also move as many cards as you want from one column to another, providing you follow the above rule. If a column is empty (you have removed all the cards), you may put a king in the space.

When you have stopped doing this and cannot move any other cards (sometimes you will not have been able to move any at all!), pick up the remainder of the pack that you put aside at the beginning and turn the cards over one at a time. If you can place the card you have just turned up either on one of the columns or on top of one of the aces, do so. If the card cannot go anywhere, put it to the side and look at the next card.

You win by getting all the cards from the columns and the remainder of the pack on to the ace piles.

HINTS
Keep your eyes open at all times! As you are placing cards from the remainder of the pack on to the columns, you may be able to move cards from one column to another or on to the ace piles. You can only go through the remainder pile twice though, so watch out!

Matchwords

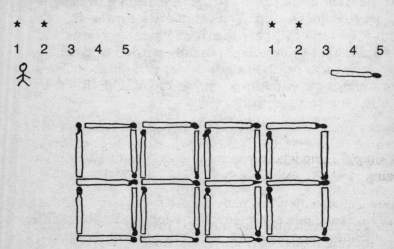

An interesting game that should be played with 'dead' matches only.

RULES
Place the matches on a table as shown above. The idea of the game is to spell out words by removing some of the matches. There are hundreds of words that you can make.

HINTS
Most words can be made if you remove between five and eleven matches.

Monte Carlo

★ ★   ★   ★   ★

1   2   3   4   5   1   2   3   4   5

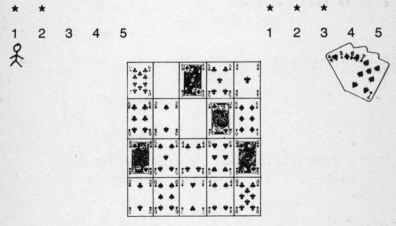

A simple game where you have to match the cards up as pairs.

RULES
Shuffle the pack and deal out four rows of five cards face up, making a total of twenty. The idea of the game is

to find matching pairs of the same number. Look at the cards and when you see two which match, take the remainder of the pack and put a new card from it on to each of the matching pair. Continue playing until you cannot find any more pairs.

To win you must be able to use up all the cards in the pack.

HINTS
Try another version, by removing cards as they match and replacing them with cards from the remainder of the pack. Try to finish the game with two empty places on the end of the bottom row. Tricky!

Pentominoes

Pentominoes was created by a mathematician nearly forty years ago. You will need to make the playing pieces yourself.

RULES
Make the twelve shapes, as shown, from stiff card. (You will notice that all of the shapes are made up of five squares.) The purpose of the game is to make various shapes out of ALL of the pentominoes placed together in the correct positions.

18

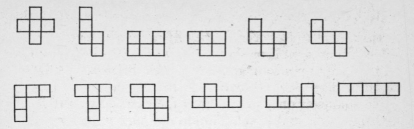

Here are some of the hundreds of different puzzles that you can try:

1 Make a rectangle of 6 squares by 10 squares.
2 Make a rectangle of 5 squares by 12 squares.
3 Make a rectangle of 4 squares by 15 squares.
4 Make a rectangle of 3 squares by 20 squares.

If you really want to test yourself, choose one of the pieces, and then use nine of the others to make a large-scale version of the piece that you chose. Very difficult, but there are solutions to the puzzle no matter which piece you choose.

HINTS
When you make a large-scale version of one of the pieces, the larger version will be three times the length and three times the height of the original piece.

Puss In The Corner

★   ★   ★   ★

1   2   3   4   5   1   2   3   4   5

Quite a simple card game that is less difficult than Klondike but equally challenging.

RULES

Take out the aces from a pack of cards and place them face up on a table as shown below. The idea of the game is to build up a sequence of cards of the same colour, red or black, by number from the aces upwards. The ace counts as one, so you must then put down a two, then a three and so on. You do not have to match the suit, just the colour, so you can put a club down on top of a spade or a diamond on top of a heart, etc.

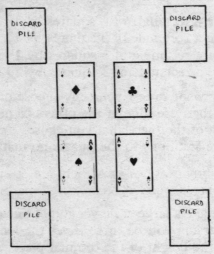

Take the remaining 48 cards (a full set without the aces), and deal them out one at a time so that they build up in four piles around the aces, as shown in the diagram. If you can put the card you turn up on top of an ace then do so. If not, put it on to one of the four discard piles. If you can put the top card from a discard pile on top of an ace pile at any stage, do so. Once all the remaining cards are either on top of an ace or on a discard pile, pick up the discarded cards and play through them once more.

To win, all the cards should be placed on top of the aces.

Always try to move cards off the discard piles whenever you can. Look out for cards that you will soon be able to put on to the ace piles and make sure that you don't put a higher card on top of them or you won't be able to move them on to the ace piles when you get the chance.

Solitaire

Solitaire is a very old game. You should be able to find a version to buy quite easily. There are cheap plastic travel versions or wooden boards with marbles.

RULES
Take the centre piece out. The aim of the game is to leave only one piece on the board. To do this you need to move the pieces by jumping one piece over another that is next door to it, either backwards, forwards or sideways, and landing in the next hole (which must be empty). You can then remove the piece that you have just jumped over.

HINTS
Try to move pieces from the edges of the board as quickly as possible and always try to move towards the centre. If you really want to test yourself, try to finish the game with the last piece in the centre hole.

Tangram

★

1   2   3   4   5

Tangram is an ancient Chinese puzzle. A set of tangram pieces consists of seven shapes which form a square, as shown below.

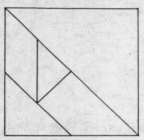

RULES

You can easily make a Tangram set for yourself by copying out the pattern shown below on to stiff card, or buy one (either wood or plastic); most toy shops sell them.

The object of the game is to arrange the pieces to form various shapes. You can make any shape you like, or try to make regular shapes such as triangles or parallelograms.

HINTS

Just use your imagination to create lots of shapes and puzzles for yourself to solve.

2 ANYTIME ANYWHERE GAMES

Buzz–Fizz

★ ★

1 2 3 4 5

★

1 2 3 4 5

This is a very silly game. It does not require anything
but a quick mind and an equally quick tongue.

RULES
The players should sit in a circle, calling out numbers
in sequence, starting from one. The next player calls
out 'two', the next 'three' and so on. Sounds easy? Here's
the catch.

If you are playing BUZZ, then the word 'Buzz' should
be called out instead of the number five or any multiple
of five (such as 10, 15, 20 and so on). 50 should be called
out as 'Buzzty', and 51 as 'Buzzty-one'.

If you are playing FIZZ, then you do the same as in BUZZ, this time using 'Fizz' for seven and multiples of seven.

Any player calling out a number when he should have called out 'Buzz' or 'Fizz' drops out. The last player left is the winner.

HINTS
Try playing BUZZ and FIZZ at the same time. Also, why not try changing from BUZZ to FIZZ or FIZZ to BUZZ half-way through a game.

Fingers

*

1 2 3 4 5

*

1 2 3 4 5

This is a very simple guessing game. You could use this to decide who gets to do the washing-up!

RULES
The idea of the game is to try to guess the total number of fingers, from none to ten, chosen by the two players.

Each player hides a hand behind his or her back. The players then show the hand, both at exactly the same time, with any number of fingers from none to five. At the same time as showing your hand you shout out the *total* number of fingers that you think will be shown by both of you – that is, the number you will show added to the number you think the other player will show. You should decide the number of rounds to be played first.

If you both guess the same number of fingers and are correct, replay that round. Note that a clenched fist is nought.

The winner is the player who guesses correctly in the most rounds.

I Went To Market

★   ★   ★   ★

1   2   3   4   5   1   2   3   4   5

A fun game that tests your vocabulary.

RULES
Each player takes it in turn to say the following: 'I went to market and bought some . . .' (The blank space should be filled with something that you can buy at the market.) The first player must think of something to buy beginning with A, the next player with B, the third with C and so on. The catch is that, on each turn, the player must run through the list of items that have already been bought, naming them in alphabetical order, before adding his own. So the first player might say, 'I went to market and bought some apples.' The second player could then continue, 'I went to market and bought some apples and some books.' The third might go on, 'I went to market and bought some apples, some books and a cauliflower.'

Any player who makes a mistake drops out and the last one left in wins.

Try playing with this sentence: 'I went to the market at . . . (a place beginning with the same letter) and bought some . . .'

Last & First

★　★　　　　　　　　　　　　★

1　2　3　4　5　　　　　　1　2　3　4　5

Another game to test your word power.

RULES

The players choose a category: towns, TV programmes or names, for example. The first player says any word from that category. The second player must call out a word which begins with the last letter of the first word. The next player then does the same, using the last letter of the second player's word, and so on. For example: London . . . Nottingham . . . Manchester . . . Reading . . . Gateshead . . . Durham, etc.

No word may be repeated. If a player cannot think of a word, or repeats a word, or calls out a word that is not in the chosen category, they drop out. The last player left in wins.

Marbles

★

1 2 3 4 5

★ ★

1 2 3 4 5

Most people have played marbles at some time. There are several different ways of playing; here is a selection.

RULES

Capture
For two players. The first player shoots a marble. The second player tries to hit the first marble. If successful, that marble is captured and the game ends. If the second player misses, then the first player shoots his marble from where it is and tries to hit the other marble. The game continues until one of the players hits the other's marble, in which case he keeps it.

Alleys
For up to four players. The first player puts a marble down on the ground some distance from the shooting line. The other players take it in turn to try to hit the target marble by shooting from behind the line. Any marbles that miss the target are kept by the owner of the target marble. When a player hits the target, he places a marble down as the new target marble.

Hundreds
For two players. Draw a small circle on the ground with chalk. Both players attempt to roll their marble into the circle. If both are successful they shoot again. When a player rolls a marble into the circle, he scores ten points. He should continue shooting marbles at the circle,

scoring ten points each time one lands there, until he either misses or has scored 100 points. If he scores 100 points, he has won. When he misses, the other player shoots. The first player to reach 100 points wins and may keep the other player's marble.

Spoof

A game of bluff. Each player must try to guess the total number of objects that are hidden in the hands of all the players.

RULES
Each player takes three small objects, such as coins, which will fit into his clenched fist. Players can decide how many objects they will hide in their hands (from one to three).

Each player must try to guess how many objects are hidden in total – that is, in all of the players' hands. Each must choose a different number. The player who guesses closest to the correct number wins that round.

HINTS
This game is more skilful than you would at first think, and calls for a logical approach.

Stone/Paper/Scissors

★

1 2 3 4 5

★

1 2 3 4 5

Different versions of this game are played throughout the world.

RULES

Each player hides a hand behind his back. Both players reveal their hands, at exactly the same time, to represent one of the following:

Scissors – two fingers forming a V
Paper – a flat hand
Stone – a clenched fist

The winner is decided by the following: scissors cut paper (scissors win), paper wraps stone (paper wins), stone blunts scissors (stone wins). If both players choose the same, neither wins. You should decide how many rounds you are going to play before you start.

HINTS

If you can try to figure out any sequence that your opponent is using, you might be able to predict his next choice.

Taboo

★ ★ ★   ★ ★

1   2   3   4   5   1   2   3   4   5

A difficult game if you haven't got your wits about you!

RULES
One of the players is made the umpire and decides which
are the taboo words in the game (that is, the words you
must not use), and how many there will be. The choice
should be words like 'yes', 'no' or 'the'. The umpire
then asks each of the players a question in turn. They
must answer without using any of the taboo words and
their sentence must make sense.

The last player to survive the questioning without using
any of the taboo words is the winner.

HINTS
Try playing the game with a letter of the alphabet as the
taboo. This way none of the players' answers may
contain that letter!

Twenty Questions

★ ★   ★ ★

1   2   3   4   5   1   2   3   4   5

Also known as 'Animal, Vegetable, Mineral', this is a perfect game to play at any time if you have lots of players.

RULES
One player picks an object that is either animal (any living creature), vegetable (any kind of plant) or mineral (everything else) and keeps it secret. The other players take it in turn to ask a question (no more than twenty in total) to try to find out what the object is. The question must be put so that the answer is either 'yes' or 'no'.

If all the twenty questions are used and the object has not been guessed, the player who thought of the object tells the others what it was and picks another. If one of the player guesses the object, he chooses one of his own and the game continues.

HINTS
If you think you have guessed the object, you can ask, 'Is it a . . . ?' Remember, though, that this counts as a question – so don't start guessing until you have enough clues.

Word Association

★

1   2   3   4   5

★   ★

1   2   3   4   5

A very interesting and simple game. Playing this will tell you a lot about your friends and their deepest thoughts!

RULES

The first player says the first word that comes into his mind. The next player says the first word that comes into *his* mind, linked to the first word. Then the next player responds to the second word and so on.

If a player hesitates, he is out of the game. The last player left in is the winner.

For example:

'Foot . . . Ball (link – the game) . . . Kick (link – the game) . . . Punch (link – fighting),' etc.

HINTS

Blank out your mind and be truthful.

3 DICE CARD AND DOMINO GAMES

Beetle

★

1 2 3 4 5

★

1 2 3 4 5

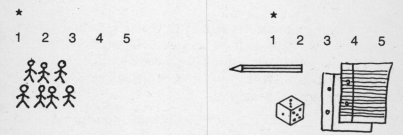

A very popular dice game. The idea is to be the first to draw a beetle. Don't worry if you can't draw.

RULES
The aim is to draw out the shape of a beetle as shown below. Each player takes it in turn to throw a dice. The

numbers on the dice represent the following parts of the beetle's body:

1 – body
2 – head
3 – one leg
4 – one eye
5 – one feeler
6 – the tail

For a player to begin, he must throw a one, which gives him the body. After that he may add any of the other parts of the beetle when the appropriate number is thrown, although the feelers or eyes cannot be drawn until the head has been got.

The winner is the first player to draw a complete beetle.

HINTS
Try playing the game for points. When a player has finished his beetle, he scores thirteen points. When it is his turn again, he starts a new beetle. The first player to score 52 points (four beetles) is the winner.

Chase The Ace

★ ★

1 2 3 4 5

This game is also known as Ranter-Go-Round, a very simple but fast card game.

RULES

Each player is given three counters and is then dealt a card, face down. The idea of the game is to get rid of a low card you might have by swapping it with another player. Each player in turn looks at his card and decides whether to keep it or swap it. In this game the ace counts as a one and is the lowest card in the pack.

Each player has two choices; he either says 'STAND', which means he wants to keep his card, or he says 'EXCHANGE', which means he wants to swap the card with the player to his left. The play continues until all the players have either kept their original card or have swapped it. The dealer can swap with the top card from the remainder of the pack. He is not allowed to swap with the next player to his left, since this person has already played once.

All the cards are now turned face up and the player with the lowest card loses a counter. In the event of a draw, the players with the lowest cards both lose a counter. When a player has lost all three of his counters he is out.

The last player left is the winner.

HINTS

Try playing the variant where if a player has a king, he turns it face up at the start of the round and the player before him cannot demand an 'Exchange' with him.

Cheat

★ ★ ★   ★ ★

1 2 3 4 5   1 2 3 4 5

Cheat is all about lying and bluffing! It should be played very quickly – the faster the better.

RULES

Shuffle the pack of cards and then deal it out to the players. If some players get more cards than others it doesn't matter.

The idea of the game is to get rid of all the cards in your hand.

The first player puts a card face down in the centre of the table and calls out what it is. The next player then puts a card down which must be the next one up in value. In other words, if the first player puts down a two, the next must put down a three and so on. When you get to the king, the ace comes next, then the two and so on.

Now for the 'cheat' part of the game. You don't have to tell the truth about the card that you have just played. In fact you can play any card you like and call it whatever you want. If you think that a player is lying about the card he has put down, you can challenge by calling out 'CHEAT'. If the player *has* cheated (that is, put down a card of a different value from what he said it was), he must pick up all the cards from the centre of the table. If the challenger was wrong and the player accused was not cheating, then the challenger must pick up all the cards.

The winner is the first player to get rid of all his cards.

HINTS
Good Cheat players are those who can look innocent when they are cheating, and very guilty when they are not!

Donkey

★ ★ ★   ★

1 2 3 4 5   1 2 3 4 5

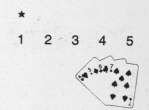

A game with a difference. No winners: just a loser. Very fast and fun.

RULES
From a full pack of cards take out one set of four cards of the same value (for example all the nines) for each player (that is, for four players take out four sets).

Put the rest of the pack aside. Shuffle the sets and deal out all the cards to the players. The idea of the game is to get a set of four cards of the same value.

Each player looks at his hand of cards, discards one of

them and passes it face down to the next player. This continues until one of the players has four cards of the same value. As soon as this happens, the player who has the complete set puts them face up on the table and touches his nose. The other players must then put a finger on their nose immediately. The last one to do so is the donkey.

When a player has been donkey six times he must make a noise like a donkey! He has then lost and drops out of the game.

HINTS
You need to be flexible about the four cards you are trying to collect, especially if you only have two the same. Be ready to change from collecting one set to another as you see what cards are being passed to you.

Drop Dead

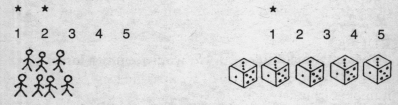

A game of luck, better with more than two players.

RULES
The first player rolls five dice. He scores the total thrown on all the dice added together. However if any show a 2 or a 5 he scores nothing, and must put aside the dice showing those numbers. He then rolls the remaining dice, again adding up the total thrown unless a 2 or 5 comes up (in which case he again scores nothing). He
38

continues in this way, scoring or discarding his dice as appropriate, and ends his turn when the last dice is discarded. The next player then takes his turn.

The player with the highest score wins.

HINTS
You'll probably need a piece of paper to keep the scores.

Old Maid

★ ★

1   2   3   4   5

★ ★

1   2   3   4   5

You can buy sets of Old Maid cards, but a normal pack of cards, with one queen removed, is just as good.

RULES
There are no winners in this game, just a loser. The idea is to get rid of all your cards by matching up pairs of numbers from any suit (aces, fives, jacks, etc.). The player who is left with the odd queen is the loser.

Remove one queen and deal out the rest of the pack. Each player then matches up any pairs that he may have and discards them.

The dealer then shows his cards to the next player only, who chooses one and takes it. If he can make a pair, he discards them. He then offers his hand to the next player in the same way and so on.

39

The game continues until all the cards have been paired up and discarded. One player will be left with the odd queen, which is called the Old Maid, and is the loser.

HINTS
Always try to pair up a queen as soon as possible, otherwise you might get stuck with it later and, of course, lose the game.

Pig

A simple dice game – but don't throw a one!

RULES
Each player in turn throws the dice and scores the amount shown on the dice. A player may continue to throw as many times as he wants, aiming to score a total of 101, though he may stop throwing whenever he chooses. He should then pass the dice to the next player and make a note of his score so far.

Should any player throw a one, he loses all the points he has scored in that turn and must pass the dice straight to the next player.

The first player to score a total of 101 or more points is the winner.

HINTS

Don't be greedy. If you have a good score (ten to fifteen isn't bad), stop and let the next player have a go – otherwise sooner or later you are going to throw a one and lose the lot!

Round The Clock

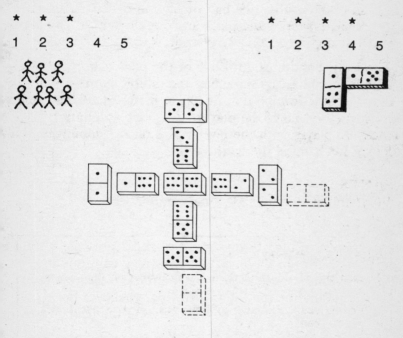

A clever domino game that needs a good deal of skill and a little luck.

RULES

Each player takes a hand of dominoes (that is, seven each for two players, six each for three players, five each for four or five players). The player who has the double-six starts. If none of the players has the double-six then each player takes another domino from the unused pile, until the double-six is found.

The player with the double-six places it face up on the table. The next player places a domino with a six on it next to the double-six. If he cannot go, then he should take a domino from the unused pile. The first four dominoes to be played must all be put against the double-six (in other words, one half of each must have a six on it). Next, players must place any double next to any of the four dominoes already placed.

The game continues until one of the players gets rid of all his dominoes, by matching the double number with one half of a domino that he has in his hand. If the game is blocked (none of the players can place a domino), then the player with the fewest pips on the dominoes left in his hand is the winner.

HINTS
Very similar to playing ordinary dominoes.

NOTES ON DOMINOES

At each end of a domino there are a number of 'pips' (dots), ranging from nought (blank) to six.

The basic idea is to match up pairs of numbers (that is, two fives, two blanks and so on).

When matched, the dominoes are placed together end to end so that the pair of numbers are next to each other. In the basic game this produces a line of dominoes to which new ones may be added at either end. The first player to get rid of all his dominoes is the winner.

Shut The Box

Originally a French game. You can buy a special wooden tray to throw the dice in, together with a row of numbers with sliding lids. You can easily play the game without these, though.

RULES

First draw nine boxes in a line as shown below, numbering the boxes from 1 to 9. You will also need nine coins or buttons.

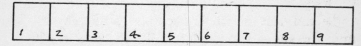

The first player throws two dice and adds the score together. He then chooses numbered squares which add up to the total score of the two dice and places a coin in each. For example, if a player throws a 3 and a 6, he may cover up the 3 and 6, or the 1 and 8, or the 2 and 7, or the 1, 3 and 5, or the 9. The player rolls again and keeps rolling as long as he can use up the total thrown each time.

When all the numbers above six in the boxes have been covered, the player may choose to throw just one dice. If he is unable to use up the score (that is, there aren't enough squares left uncovered), he must finish his turn and the remaining uncovered numbers are added together to give his score.

43

When all the players have had a turn, the one with the lowest score is the winner.

HINTS
Try to cover up the highest numbers first.

Snip, Snap, Snorem

★   ★ ★

1 2   3   4   5   1   2   3   4   5

A card game all about matching.

RULES
Shuffle and deal the whole pack out to the players. The aim of the game is to get rid of all the cards in your hand.

The first player places a card of his choice face up on the table. The second player must try to play a card of the same value (for example, the seven of hearts has the same value as the seven of clubs). If he can, he places the card on top of the first one and calls out 'Snip'. The third player then has a go, and if he can place a card, he says 'Snap'. The next player, if he too can lay a card of the same value, does so and says 'Snorem'. The four cards are put to one side and the player who placed the 'Snorem' card begins a new round, playing any card he likes.

If a player does not have a card of the same value as the last one played, he must say 'pass' and miss a go.

44

The winner is the player who gets rid of all his cards first.

HINTS
When choosing a card to begin a round, always try to pick a value of which you have more than one. This will ensure that at least one of the other players will miss a go. Remember, though, that they will be doing the same!

4 BOARD GAMES

Achi

★ ★

1 2 3 4 5

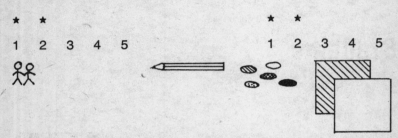

1 2 3 4 5

Achi is a game that is played by Ghanian children. It is rather like Noughts and Crosses, but with one major difference – you can move your noughts and crosses around!

RULES
Make the board as shown below. You will need four counters each. The object of the game is to get three counters in a line, just like in noughts and crosses. The

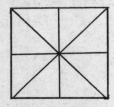

two players take it in turn to place one of their counters on an empty point (that is, where two or three lines meet, or at the centre). When the eight pieces have been placed, each player may move one of his pieces along a line to another empty point.

The first player to get three counters in a row (either down, across or diagonally) wins.

HINTS
Don't worry too much about having a counter on the centre point.

Draughts

★　★　★　★　　　　　　　★　★　★

1　2　3　4　5　　　　　　1　2　3　4　5

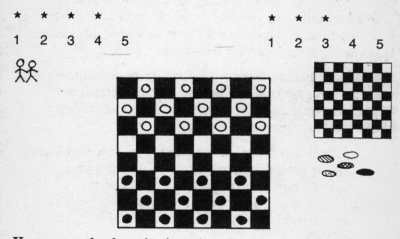

Known as checkers in America, Draughts has many variants throughout the world. The version below is the British/American one.

RULES
Each player sets up his twelve playing pieces at either end of the board on the white squares of the first three

rows of squares (as shown in the illustration). The black player plays first, then the white and so on. Pieces may only be moved forward, diagonally, into an empty square and only into the white squares, *never* the black.

You can capture one of your opponent's pieces by jumping over it into an empty square. If you manage to jump over an opponent's piece, remove it from the board. You may capture as many pieces as you can. (If you can make a series of jumps in one turn and therefore capture several pieces, then do so.) Remember that in this first stage of the game your pieces can only move forwards.

When one of your pieces reaches the far end of the board, that piece becomes a 'king'. Take one of the pieces that have been captured and removed from the board and put it on top of the 'king' piece. 'King' pieces move in exactly the same way as normal pieces, except that they can move either forwards *or* backwards.

The winner is the player who either removes all the other player's pieces, or blocks him so that he cannot move. There are some additional rules to the game which you should try to remember:

1 If you can jump an opponent's pieces, you must do so even if you are likely to lose the jumping piece when your opponent has his turn.
2 If you spot a jumping move that your opponent has missed then you can insist that he makes that move.
3 You should take no longer than five minutes to make a move.

HINTS
Try playing touch and move; if a player touches a piece (if he is thinking of moving it but changes his mind),

he *must* move it. Draughts may look easy, but it is considered to be as difficult as Chess to play well. There are international Draughts championships, where the skill of the players is very high.

Fox & Geese

★ ★   ★   ★   ★
1 2   3   4   5   1   2   3   4   5

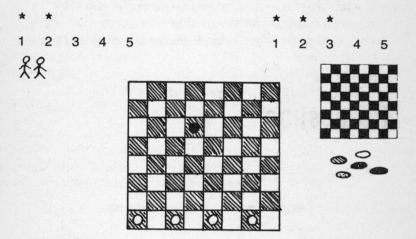

There are various versions of Fox and Geese. This one can be played on a normal chess- or draughts-board.

RULES
Set the counters up as shown. There are four Geese pieces, which are placed on the back line of black squares. The one Fox piece may be placed in any other black square on the board.

The two players move alternately. The Geese player moves first. He may only move his pieces forward, diagonally, just like in draughts, although they may not jump over pieces, since blocking is central to the game. The Fox player also moves diagonally, but can move forwards or backwards.

49

The Geese player wins if he can block the Fox player so that he cannot move. The Fox player wins if he can break through the line of Geese and get to the far end of the board.

HINTS

There is a definite strategy to Fox & Geese but if we told you what it is, it would spoil the game for you! We would recommend, however, that Fox players who are new to this game place their piece as far away as possible from the Geese.

Horseshoe

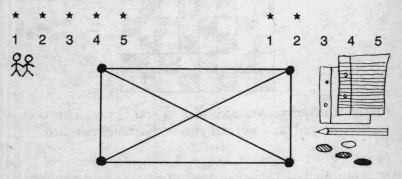

Horseshoe is an ancient game which is very popular in China, where it is called Png Hau K'i. Fortunately it is easier to play than to say!

RULES
Draw up the board as shown. Each player starts with two counters set up as illustrated. The idea of the game is to move your counters along the lines and block your opponent's pieces so that they cannot move. The first

player moves one of his pieces into the centre; the second player can then move one of his pieces into the empty space the other player just left.

The play continues until you block your opponent or he blocks you.

HINTS
Try designing a board to play with three pieces each. The three-piece version is called Madelinette.

Kono

A clever game; you need to have your wits about you to play this well.

RULES
Make a board as shown below. The idea of the game is to capture all of your opponent's pieces or block them so that they cannot move.

Take it in turns to move. To capture one of your opponent's pieces you must jump over one of your own pieces and land on one of your opponent's (for example, a black piece jumps over another black piece, lands on a white one and captures it). You can only move along a line, therefore diagonal moves are impossible. The piece that you land on is removed from play.

If you cannot move one of your pieces so that it lands on one of your opponent's, then you can move a piece directly along a line from one point to another empty one.

HINTS
Don't be too hasty. There are lots of choices once both players have lost two pieces. Think about your strategy then, because the game really starts after that.

Mancala

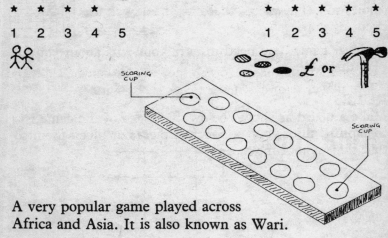

A very popular game played across Africa and Asia. It is also known as Wari.

RULES
The board is rather odd; it consists of shallow holes carved into a block of wood. Alternatively, you can use

twelve saucers or draw the two rows of six 'holes' on a
piece of paper, and add scoring cups. For the counters,
use either coins, buttons or small stones.

Start the game with four playing pieces in each of the
holes. The first player picks up all the pieces from one
of the holes on his side of the board. He then 'sows' (or
drops) one of the pieces into each of the next holes anti-
clockwise. The second player then does the same with
the pieces from one of the holes on his side of the board.

If a hole has more than twelve pieces, then these will go
round more than one circuit of the board. In this case
the empty hole is missed out when 'sowing'.

If the last counter put into a hole is on the opponent's
side of the board and that hole contains only two or three
pieces (not four), then the player wins those pieces and
the ones in the holes on either side of it, providing that
there are only two or three pieces (not four) in those
holes too. The pieces that have been won are put in a
scoring cup.

The game continues until there are no counters left on
one side of the board (or no more seeds can be captured).
The player who has most pieces is the winner.

Nine Holes

★ ★ ★   ★ ★

1 2 3 4 5   1 2 3 4 5

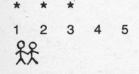   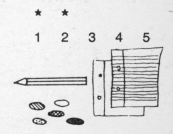

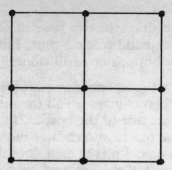

Similar to Achi (*see* p. 46), but each player starts with three pieces instead of four.

RULES

Make a board as shown. Each player takes it in turn to place one of their three counters on the board at one of the points where two or more lines join. The aim of the game is to get three pieces in a row. Once all the pieces are placed, take it in turns to move one of your pieces from one point to another empty one next door to it.

The first player to get three in a row is the winner.

HINTS

Don't rely on the same tactics you use for Noughts and Crosses; they won't work!

Nine Men's Morris

★ ★ ★

1 2 3 4 5

★ ★ ★

1 2 3 4 5

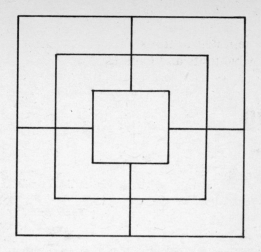

This is a very old game; you can buy a proper set, but it is quite easy to make one.

RULES

First of all make the board as shown. At the start of a game, each player has nine 'men' or counters. Taking it in turn, each player puts one counter on one of the points on the board (where two or more lines join). The aim is to get three counters in a row. If a player can manage this, he can remove one of his opponent's pieces from the board.

Once all the pieces are on the board, the players take it in turns to move a piece from one point on the board to another empty one that is next door to it and joined directly by a line. Every time a player gets three counters in a row, he removes another enemy counter.

When one player leaves the other with just two counters, or when his opponent is blocked and cannot move, he is the winner.

HINTS
Don't be tempted to think that this is just a jazzed-up version of Noughts and Crosses!

Viking

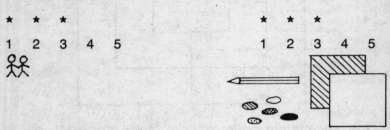

This is a very old game. It was extremely popular in northern Europe throughout the Dark Ages and was played until Chess overtook it.

RULES
First of all make up the board as shown. The aim of the game is for the black player to capture the white king; for the white player to win, he must get his king to one of the corner squares.

All pieces move in the same way, just like a rook (or castle) in Chess – that is, horizontally or vertically (up, down or across the board). Each player can move a piece as far as he likes in a straight line on each turn. Only the king can enter the king's square in the centre, or at each corner of the board.

Pieces are captured by sandwiching (that is, by having two of the opponent's pieces, one on either side, in next-door squares). The king's squares (all five of them) count towards sandwiching for the white side without necessarily having a piece in them.

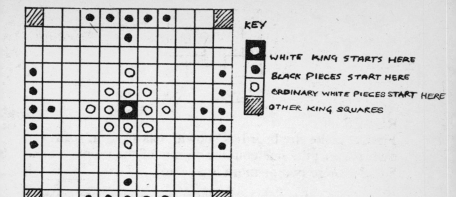

KEY

WHITE KING STARTS HERE
BLACK PIECES START HERE
ORDINARY WHITE PIECES START HERE
OTHER KING SQUARES

The black player moves first and each player may only move one piece per turn.

HINTS
This is a game of attack and defence. The white player has fewer pieces and should concentrate on being able to get his king out to the edge of the board. The black player should try to capture any stray white piece that he can.

Zulu

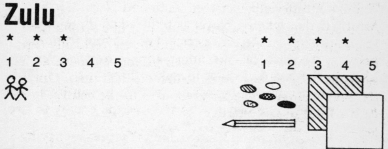

★ ★ ★

1 2 3 4 5

★ ★ ★ ★

1 2 3 4 5

This game is similar in many respects to Nine Men's Morris (*see* p. 54), but has some subtle differences. Played by the Zulu in southern Africa, it is also called Mlaba-Laba.

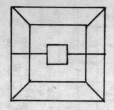

RULES

Firstly, make the board as shown. Taking it in turn, each player puts one counter on one of the points on the board (where two or more lines join).

The pieces, of which each player has twelve, are called 'black cattle' and 'brown cattle', but black and white draughts pieces can be used.

Both players place the counters on the board as in Nine Men's Morris, trying to get three in a row. If a player does so, he can remove one of his opponent's counters.

The second part of the game is also as for Nine Men's Morris, with each player moving one piece at a time from one point on the board to another. Each time three in a row are achieved, another of the opponent's counters is removed.

The main difference between Zulu and Nine Men's Morris is that when a player is reduced to three pieces in Zulu, he is no longer restricted to moving from one point to the next; he can 'jump' a piece to wherever he likes on the board, so that it makes three in a row. This is, of course, the last desperate attempt to win by a losing player. The player who reduces the enemy to two counters is the winner.

HINTS

There are more connections than in Nine Men's Morris. Make sure you don't forget the angled corner connecting lines.

5 FAMILY GAMES

Adverts

★   ★   ★   ★

1   2   3   4   5   1   2   3   4   5

A fun game that tests your powers of memory as well as showing you how effective adverts are.

RULES

Take a pile of old magazines and newspapers and cut out all the adverts you can find (twenty or so is enough). Look at each advert carefully and then cut out any mention of what is being advertised (for example the name of the product and the manufacturer).

Number the adverts and lay them out on a table where all the players can see them.

Give each player a pencil and paper and ten minutes to write down the names of the products that the advertisements are for.

The player with the most correct answers is the winner.

Try picking out a couple of really odd adverts, or just give the players a fragment of the advert; that will really test them!

Alpha

Another word-listing game. Try to come up with the longest words you can think of.

RULES
Give each player a piece of paper and a pencil. The idea of the game is for each player to think up the longest words they can. The catch is that they only have fifteen minutes to write twenty-six words, one starting with each letter of the alphabet.

The player who comes up with the longest words is the winner.

HINTS
Try playing the ultra-difficult version of Alpha where the words have to begin and end with the same letter. Here are a few to give you the idea: EveryonE, KayaK, TournamenT and WindoW.

Anagrams

* * *

1   2   3   4   5

* *

1   2   3   4   5

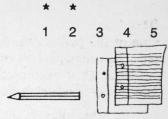

This game needs some preparation but after the hard work just sit back and watch the players sweat!

RULES

Prepare a list of jumbled up words (anagrams) which belong to the same category, for example animals or countries. Put the list where all the players can see it. Give them five or ten minutes, depending on how many words there are, to solve the anagrams.

Here are some examples:

RAEB = BEAR   KUDC = DUCK
BINOR = ROBIN   NOKMYE = MONKEY

The winner is the player with the most correct solutions.

HINTS

Try to make the anagrams look as if they are real words, which will confuse the players more.

Botticelli

* *

1   2   3   4   5

* * *

1   2   3   4   5

A simple guessing game – but you'll need to remember as many famous people as you can.

RULES
One of the players thinks of a famous person but only tells the other players the first letter of that person's surname. (For example, he might think of Jason Donovan, in which case he tells them 'D'.)

All the other players must think of someone whose name begins with that letter and take it in turns to describe this celebrity briefly to the first player, without naming them. (For example, one player might think of Paul Daniels, so he would ask the first player indirectly whether this was the person he had also thought of, perhaps by asking, 'Are you a TV magician?')

The first player must now try to guess which celebrity the other player has thought of, and answer his question by stating (if this is the case) that he is not that famous person. (In our example, he would therefore reply, 'No, I am not Paul Daniels.')

If the first player guesses correctly who the other player had in mind, then it is someone else's turn to think up a celebrity for him to guess. If he is wrong, however, the other player may then ask him a 'bonus' question to try to work out which famous person the first player had originally thought of. This question can be any for which the reply will be either 'yes' or 'no'. (For example, he could ask 'Are you a woman?', but not 'How old are you?')

Play continues in this way until someone guesses the first person's celebrity correctly.

HINTS
When you are trying to guess the first player's celebrity, think of unusual people who will be difficult for him to

get right. This will help you to get more bonus questions. Think carefully about which bonus questions to ask, as some are much more useful than others.

Categories

A great game of general knowledge.

RULES
Each player thinks of a category (for example people, countries, etc.) and everyone writes down all the categories picked. Then a letter of the alphabet is chosen and the players have ten minutes to write down as many words as they can think of beginning with that letter in each category.

When the time is up, each player reads out their list of words. Any words that have not been thought of by anyone else score one point each, but any word that is on another player's list scores nothing.

The player with the highest score is the winner.

HINTS
Try to think of odd and unusual words that you don't think other players will have thought of.

I Spy

★   ★

1   2   3   4   5   1   2   3   4   5

The classic game to play in the car; in fact, this game can be played almost anywhere!

RULES

One of the players looks around and chooses an object that he can see. The others have to try to guess what it is. The only clue that they have is the first letter of the object chosen.

The first player says: 'I spy with my little eye, something beginning with . . .' and fills in the gap at the end of the statement with the first letter of the object.

Here is an example, during a car journey:

> 'I spy with my little eye, something beginning with R.'
> 'Rain?'
> 'No.'
> 'Rover?'
> 'No.'
> 'River?'
> 'No.'
> 'Railway?'
> 'No.'
> 'Road?'
> 'Yes, your turn.'

HINTS

You can easily cheat in this game (not that we encourage that sort of thing, of course!), by changing to another word beginning with the same letter if one of the other players guesses your first word!

Picture Consequences

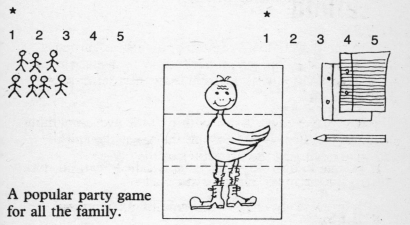

A popular party game for all the family.

RULES

Give each player a piece of paper with two lines drawn across it so that the paper is equally divided into three sections. In the top section each player draws a head, of any sort – animal, human or whatever. The neck should be drawn just over the line and the paper then folded to hide the drawing and passed on to another player. This player draws a body, again of any type; the top of the legs should just go over the line. The paper is folded again to conceal the body and passed along to a third player who draws the legs.

When the drawings have been completed the paper is unfolded and the weird creation is revealed.

HINTS
It doesn't matter how badly you draw for this game – some of the funniest 'creatures' can come from the worst drawings!

Scaffold

If anyone knows why this game is called Scaffold, please tell us!

RULES
The players are given three letters and they have ten minutes to come up with a list of words which contain all the letters. The players score one point for every word they have thought of.

The highest scorer is the winner.

Here is an example:

Letters chosen: EDT

Determine   Teddy   Tedious   Educate   Death
Thunder   Detail

HINTS

Try making it more difficult by making the players think of words that have the letters in the given order, so in the above example only EDUCATE would score them a point. Also, don't use Zs or Qs very much; there aren't many words containing either of them.

Short Story

★
1   2   3   4   5

★ ★
1   2   3   4   5

RULES

The players are given a time limit of, say, fifteen minutes to write a short story. Here's the catch: none of the words used should be more than three letters long! When the time is up all the stories are read out to the other players. The player who has made up the most amusing story is the winner.

HINTS

The story doesn't have to make much sense, but it's better if it does.

Stepping Stones

★ ★ ★   ★ ★ ★

1   2   3   4   5   1   2   3   4   5

A really good game of word association.

RULES
Each player is given, in turn, four words or themes by
the other players. He must make up one sentence for
each that somehow links it with the next, however
strange the connection! The other players are the
referees, and it is up to them to decide whether the
player has made a sensible association (or link) between
the given subjects.

Here is an example:

The player must link: the body, cars, water, predators

HANDS ARE PART OF THE *BODY*
THE *BODY* OF A CAR IS MADE OF *METAL*
IT'S THE *METALS* IN TAP WATER THAT ARE
DANGEROUS
ONE OF THE MOST *DANGEROUS* CREATURES
IN THE WORLD IS A *SHARK*

HINTS
This is not a really serious game so jokes and puns are
quite acceptable.

68

6 ALTERNATIVE
GAMES

Backward Spelling

★ ★

1 2 3 4 5

A perfect game to play any time if you have at least three players.

RULES
Taking it in turns, the players call out a word and quickly choose one of the other players to spell it. The catch is that the second player must spell it backwards, within a time limit. (This should be decided before starting the game.)

The player scores a point if he spells the word backwards correctly; if not he drops out of the game, which continues either until there is only one player left or until time is up, in which case the winner is the player with the highest score.

Be sensible; don't expect a younger player to be able to spell very long and difficult words backwards!

Crambo

★   ★ ★

1 2 3 4 5   1 2 3 4 5

A fun word game that has been popular for centuries.

RULES
One of the players thinks of a word. He then thinks of another which rhymes with it and says it out loud (for example he might think of BELL and say SMELL). The other players have five guesses to find the word that he is keeping secret. The player who guesses the word correctly chooses the next one. If none of the players have figured it out, then the first player tells them his first word and chooses another.

HINTS
Try thinking of a weird and unusual rhyming word to put the others off!

Diagonal Draughts

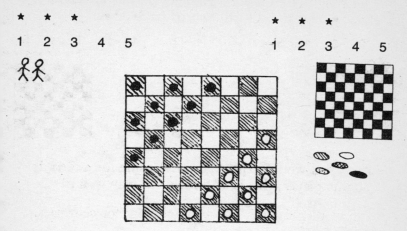

Just like ordinary Draughts but with one big difference.

RULES
The rules are exactly the same as for the ordinary game of Draughts (*see* p. 47). The major difference is that the pieces start in the corners of the board as shown. The 'king' (or crowning) squares are marked.

HINTS
As with Draughts, you can play it with either nine or twelve pieces each.

Losing Draughts

★ ★ ★

1 2 3 4 5

★ ★

1 2 3 4 5

Not, as you would expect, an ideal game for a terrible Draughts player; this is as difficult to play well as Draughts itself.

RULES
The rules are exactly the same as for ordinary Draughts (*see* p. 47), except that the winner is the first player to lose all of his pieces. A player must always jump an opponent's piece if he can. If he misses taking a piece he must go back and make his move again, this time taking his opponent's piece.

HINTS
Try to set your pieces up so that your opponent must take several of your pieces at a time. Always let him get a king, as this is to your advantage in Losing Draughts.

Suicide Chess

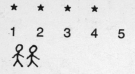

This is the chess version of Losing Draughts. You need to know how to play Chess to play this game.

RULES

All the rules of normal Chess apply, with the following exceptions: if you can take a piece, you must do so; the king is just like any other piece and may be captured.

The first player to lose all his pieces is the winner.

HINTS

There is no real strategy that can be offered to someone who already plays Chess, but try to get rid of your most powerful pieces first.

7 ACTIVITY GAMES

Balloon Race

★   ★

1 2 3 4 5   1 2 3 4 5

A fun party game that needs a big room; or you can play it in the garden as long as it's not too windy!

RULES
Each player should have a different coloured balloon. The competitors race to the far end of the room and back again. The catch is that you cannot carry the balloon – you must hit it or kick it along. If a player holds his balloon he should be sent back and should start again. The winner is the first player to complete the course.

HINTS
Are you serious?!

Blind Man's Buff

★

1 2 3 4 5

★

1 2 3 4 5

A great game if you've got plenty of players.

RULES
Choose one of the players to be the 'blind man'.
Blindfold him and put him in the middle of the room.
Spin him around a few times, then leave him.

The other players should move around the room trying
not to be caught by the blind man, but if he does touch
one of them, that player must stop and stand still. The
blind man then tries to guess who he has captured. If
he guesses correctly, then the captive becomes the blind
man. If he guesses incorrectly, then he must let go of
the captive and the game continues until someone is
caught and correctly identified.

HINTS
Try standing very still against a wall if the blind man
comes close.

Charades

★ ★

1 2 3 4 5

★ ★

1 2 3 4 5

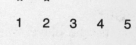

Charades is a very popular game, best played in teams.

RULES
One of the players from the team going first chooses a word that contains several syllables which form words in their own right (for example illuminate: 'ill', 'human' and 'ate'). The player must then mime each syllable in turn for the other team to guess. When they have worked out what the whole word was, one of their members must come up with a word and mime it. But if they fail to guess correctly, the first team should tell them what the word was and think of another word to mime themselves.

HINTS
Try playing the popular version where you choose TV programmes and book and film titles to mime. In this version, you can mime whole words, although you will still sometimes have to split longer words into syllables.

Goodies & Baddies

★   ★

1 2 3 4 5   1 2 3 4 5

A perfect game to let off steam.

RULES
Divide the players into two teams. One team are the Goodies. They must try to keep a balloon up in the air. The other team, the Baddies, must try to burst it. It is

forbidden to use anything except hands and feet to do this.

When the balloon has been burst, the teams swap around. The Goodies become the Baddies and try to burst the second balloon.

HINTS
Pins are definitely out!

Hot & Cold

The classic party game.

RULES
One player leaves the room. The other players hide a small object somewhere. When the first player is called back into the room, he must hunt for the object, while the others shout out 'very cold . . . cold . . . warm . . . hot . . . very hot' according to how close he gets to the object. (The closer he gets, the 'warmer' he is.)

Each player should have a turn at trying to find the object, which will obviously be hidden in a different place each time.

HINTS
Look for the object in a systematic way, rather than rushing from one side of the room to the other. This makes it easier to follow the clues the other players are giving you.

Hunt The Thimble

A very simple game that is ideal for younger children.

RULES
One player stays in the room and puts an object (that has been shown to the other players first) somewhere in the room. It should not be hidden, but should not be too obvious either. The other players are called back into the room and try to find the object. When one of them spots it they should sit down and keep quiet. The last one to spot the object is the loser.

HINTS
Don't give it away when you find out where the object has been put.

Murder In the Dark

A great party game.

RULES

Tear up sheets of paper so you have one piece for each player. On one of the pieces draw a circle and on another draw a cross. Fold up all the slips, jumble them up and give one to each player.

The player who gets the circle is the detective and should let the rest of the players know this. The player who gets the cross is the murderer and should not declare himself to the others.

All the lights in the house are turned off and the players scatter around and hide. The murderer must then try to find a victim. He whispers 'You're dead' to his victim, who must then scream as the murderer runs away.

As soon as he hears the scream, the detective can switch on the lights and run to the scene of the crime. He then calls everyone together and questions them. Everyone must answer truthfully except the murderer who can lie. The detective, if he thinks he has the right man, can ask outright, 'Are you the murderer?' If he has guessed right, the murderer must confess. If he is wrong, the detective only has one more guess.

HINTS

Try not to look guilty if you are the murderer, and don't hesitate when questioned. The detective can ask outright if a player is the murderer, but without any clues this is a bit chancy. Remember that after two wrong guesses the detective has lost the game.

Try asking questions that a real detective would ask, like . . . 'Where were you at the time of the murder?' and so on.

Musical Islands

★　　　　　　　　　　　　　★

1　2　3　4　5　　　　　　1　2　3　4　5

RULES
Sheets of newspaper are placed on the floor around the room. The players then walk around the room while the music plays and when it stops, they must try to get on the islands of newspaper. More than one player can occupy an island, but if a player fails to get on to one because there is no space left, then he is out.

The number of islands should be reduced gradually, by taking away a piece of newspaper after each 'round'. The last remaining player on an island is the winner.

HINTS
Keep your eyes and ears open.

Newspaper Race

★　　　　　　　　　　　　　★

1　2　3　4　5　　　　　　1　2　3　4　5

A fast and furious game; you need an umpire for this.

RULES
Each player should have two sheets of newspaper. The competitors line up at one end of the room and the idea is to be first to get to the other end of the room and back. The players have to use the two sheets of newspaper as stepping stones, putting one down on the ground, stepping on it and then putting the second one in front and moving on to that one, and so on across the room.

If any player touches the floor, he must go back to the start and begin again.

HINTS
Don't try picking up a sheet of paper while you're standing on it! Also, it's more challenging to play with small sheets than large ones.

Squeak Piggy, Squeak

★

1 2 3 4 5

★

1 2 3 4 5

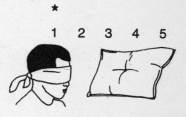

A bit like Blind Man's Buff, but you have to make silly noises as well.

RULES
One of the players is blindfolded, given a cushion and spun around two or three times. All the other players sit down on chairs in a circle around him. The blindfolded

player has to put the cushion on the lap of one of the seated players and then sit down on it.

The blindfolded player than says, 'Squeak Piggy, Squeak', and the player whose knee he is sitting on squeals like a pig. The blindfolded player has to guess who it is and if he is right, the squeaker must swap places with him. If he is wrong, he has to find another lap to sit on and must guess again.

HINTS
Don't forget to swap seats whenever there is a new blindfolded player, otherwise he'll know exactly who is where.

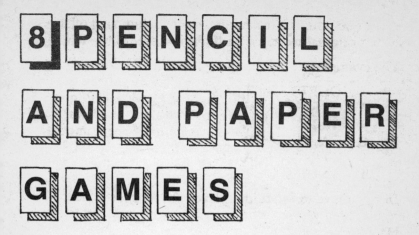

8 PENCIL AND PAPER GAMES

Acrostics

RULES

Give a piece of paper and a pencil to each of the players. Choose a six- or seven-letter word which each player must then write down the left-hand side of the page, in a column (so that each letter is underneath the one before it). Then write the same word, with the letters in reverse order, down the right-hand side of the page, also in a column.

The players then have five minutes to think of the longest word they can which begins with a letter on the left and ends with the corresponding letter on the right. They score one point for each letter (not including the letters of the original word). The highest scorer is the winner.

For example:

T	OURIS	T
A	GRE	E
R	AISIN	G
G	EA	R
E	XTR	A
T	ANGEN	T

In the above example the player scores 23.

HINTS
Try to avoid words that contain too many of the same letters, like MISSISSIPPI!

Battleships

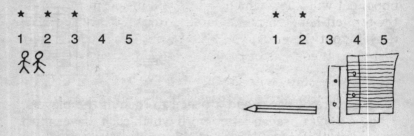

Said to have been invented by British prisoners of war held in Germany during the First World War (1914–18).

RULES
Each of the two players marks out two identical grids on his piece of paper as shown below, numbering them vertically (down) 1 to 10 and horizontally (across) A to

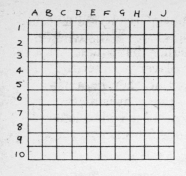

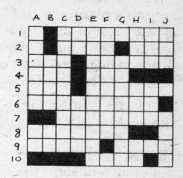

J. It is much easier to use graph paper as this means that you don't have to draw out the grids every time.

By numbering and lettering the grid, you can then call out a number and a letter (for example A1) and the opponent will know which square you mean (in this case, the top left-hand corner square). After you have finished drawing out the grids, you need to put your fleet on the first grid; it consists of the following ships:

1 Battleship (four squares in a line across or down)
2 Cruisers (three squares each in a line across or down)
3 Destroyers (two squares each in a line across or down)
4 Submarines (one square each)

Now colour in the squares that you have chosen for your ships on the first grid. There must be at least one empty square between each ship. When both players have done this, the game begins. The aim of the game is to sink the enemy fleet.

Each player takes it in turns to fire a shot by calling out the number of a square (for example F3). The opponent looks at his first grid and sees whether that square has a ship on it. He must tell the other player whether the shot was a hit or a miss. If it was a hit, then he must say what sort of ship it was. The other player then records either a miss (with an M) or a hit with a letter corresponding to the type of ship hit (in other words a B, C, D or S) on his second grid.

The players continue firing until one person's fleet has been sunk.

HINTS
Don't put your ships too close together.

Boxes

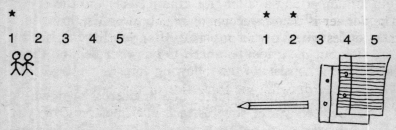

A simple game that needs a lot of concentration not to miss opportunities.

RULES
Draw ten rows of ten dots on a piece of paper, as shown below.

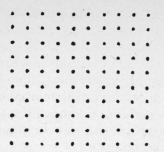

The players take it in turns to connect two of the dots (by drawing a line between them), vertically or horizontally (down or across). The idea of the game is to make as many boxes as possible. A box is made by drawing in the fourth and last side of the square. When a player finishes a box he puts his initials in it. He can then draw another line and if this finishes another box all the better. The player continues until a line that he draws does not finish a box, when it is his opponent's turn again.

The winner is the player whose initials appear in the most boxes when all the dots have been joined.

HINTS

Try to avoid drawing the third side of a square. If you do, your opponent will score on his next turn.

Bulls & Cows

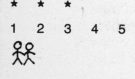

★   ★   ★

1   2   3   4   5

★   ★   ★   ★

1   2   3   4   5

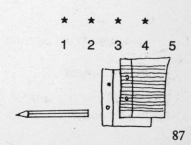

An apparently simple game that can actually be quite difficult.

RULES

One of the players thinks of a four-digit number. The other player has to guess what the number is. The player who thought of the number must give the guesser clues, which he does by letting the guesser know whether any of the digits in the number he has guessed are correct, or are in the right places. If the guesser has chosen a number that has a correct digit in the right place, this is called a bull; if he has chosen a correct digit but in the wrong place, it is called a cow.

The first player should not give away which digits are right, but should just say how many bulls or cows his opponent has scored.

For example, a game might go like this:

NUMBER CHOSEN: 7649

First guess:	8555	nothing
Second guess:	4999	one bull (the last 9, correct number in the correct place), one cow (the 4 is a correct digit in the wrong place)
Third guess:	5679	two bulls, one cow (the 6 and 9 are bulls and the 7 is a cow)
Fourth guess:	6679	two bulls
Fifth guess:	7779	two bulls
Sixth guess:	7759	two bulls
Seventh guess:	7649	four bulls

When the mystery number has been guessed, the players swap places and the guesser thinks of a number. The winner is the player to have made fewest guesses before working out the number correctly.

HINTS
Make sure that you write down all the combinations that you have called out, also noting whether you got any cows or bulls for each one. This will help you to work out which digits are correct and which are not.

Combinations

A game that really tests your word power.

RULES
Make a list of ten two- or three-letter combinations (for example OLY or EST). Then, setting a time limit of five minutes, the two players must come up with the longest words they can think of containing these letter combinations. (For example, using EST, your word could be STRANGEST.) The players score one point for each letter used in addition to the combinations.

If you had chosen the letter combinations shown below in capitals, here are some words you might come up with, and the scores they would make:

     strangEST   = 6
     hUNGry   = 3
     KangeROO   = 5

PERfection	= 7
cOUNtries	= 5
horseSHOe	= 6
ABRoad	= 3
NAUghty	= 4
tidDLYwinks	= 9
scrAMBled	= 6
TOTAL SCORE	= 54

HINTS

Don't choose a combination like XKP. Can you think of a word containing those letters?! Three-letter combinations will usually need to contain at least one vowel.

Crosswords

*   *   *

1   2   3   4   5

*   *   *

1   2   3   4   5

This game is rather like Scrabble*, but you can choose any letters you like to make up your words.

RULES

Draw out a grid (or use graph paper) nine squares by nine. The first player writes a word on to the grid, one letter per box, and scores one point for each letter. The

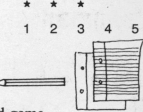

I	M	P	A	T	I	E	N	T

I	M	P	A	T	I	E	N	T
	R							R
T	R	I	C	K				E
	N		N		W	O	E	
			C	H	A	I	R	
	E		C			I		
			K			S		
						T		
						S		

second player must then write down a word which interlocks with the first word, like a crossword puzzle. He also scores one point for each letter. Play continues until neither player can add a word to the grid. The player with most points wins.

HINTS
Always try to start the game with a nine-letter word, as this is the best opportunity to get a high score.

*'Scrabble' is a trademark of Spears Games

Guggenheim

★ ★

1   2   3   4   5

★   ★   ★

1   2   3   4   5

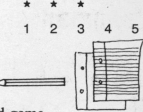

Guggenheim is another classic word game.

RULES
A list of six categories is chosen, such as towns, birds,

countries, colours, TV programmes and clothes. Each player writes these down on the left-hand side of his sheet of paper. Then the players choose a keyword which can be any word of five or more letters. This is written along the top of the page, with the letters spaced out. The players have ten minutes to come up with a word from each category on the left that starts with each of the letters from the keyword. The player with the most words, or the longest words, is the winner.

For example:

	S	P	A	C	E
Towns	Skegness	Portsmouth	Aberdeen	Carlisle	Edinburgh
Birds	Seagull	Pigeon	Albatross	Cormorant	Eagle
Countries	Sweden	Portugal	Albania	Canada	Egypt
Colours	Sepia	Pink	Amber	Cream	Earth
TV Shows	Scooby Doo	Pob	Alas Smith and Jones	Cosby Show	EastEnders
Clothes	Scarf	Pinny	Apron	Cardigan	Evening Dress

HINTS
Don't pick a keyword which has any letters repeated.

Hangman

★

1 2 3 4 5

★ ★

1 2 3 4 5

92

A great word-guessing game.

RULES
One player picks a word with six or more letters. He then draws a series of dashes on a piece of paper to represent the letters of the word. (For example, if he chooses CRICKET, then he puts down – – – – – – –.) The other player must guess the word by choosing letters, one at a time. If he guesses correctly, then the first player writes in the letter on the appropriate dash. If he guesses wrongly, then the player jots down the letter and draws one of the lines in the hangman picture, as shown below. The guesser can only make eleven mistakes before he is hanged and loses the game ('hangman' is made up of eleven lines).

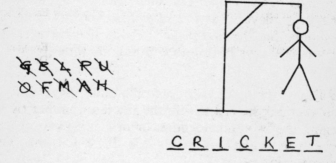

When the guesser has worked out the word, it is his turn to think up one. If he loses and is hanged, the first player chooses another word.

HINTS
Words with letters repeated are much easier to guess.

Snake

★   ★ ★

1 2 3 4 5   1 2 3 4 5

Similar in some respects to Boxes (*see* p. 87), this is a skilful little game; you need to keep your wits about you.

RULES
Draw out ten rows of ten dots, just as for Boxes. The first player draws a line connecting two of the dots; this is the start of the snake. Diagonal lines are not allowed. The second player draws another line, starting from one of the dots that the first player joined. The players take it in turns, always having to continue the line (from either side).

The idea of the game is to force the other player into a position where he has to join the snake up, either by bringing the two ends together or by joining one end to another part of the continuous line. If he does this, he loses the game.

HINTS
Always keep your eyes open. Don't get so concerned with blocking your opponent at one end that you ignore the other.

Sprouts

★ ★   ★   ★   ★

1   2   3   4   5   1   2   3   4   5

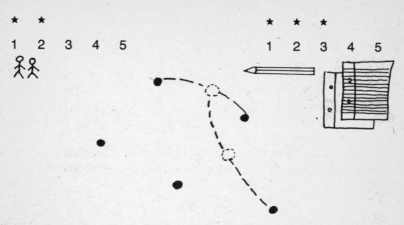

This game was invented in the 1960s; since then, millions of people have played it. It looks very simple, but needs a lot of concentration to play well.

RULES
Draw five dots on a sheet of paper. The players take it in turns to join up two of the dots and put a new dot somewhere on the line that has been drawn.

Sounds simple enough? Here are the catches: no line may cross another line; no line may pass through an existing dot; no dot may have more than three lines coming out of it.

The players continue until no more lines can be drawn. The player who draws the last line is the winner.

HINTS
When drawing a line at the beginning of the game, try to make sure that you link up the dots that are furthest away from each other. Be careful about *where* you place the dot on the line that you have just drawn. Always

try to use up all three of the lines allowed from a dot as quickly as possible, as this will restrict where your opponent can draw a line.

Stairs

A great game that will really test your vocabulary.

RULES
The players decide on a letter of the alphabet. They have ten minutes to come up with a 'stair' of words which starts with that letter, each word containing one more letter than the previous one. The letter is written at the top of the page. The stair consists of a two-letter word, then a three-letter word, then a four-letter word and so on. The player with the longest stair is the winner.

I
IN
INN
ICES
IGLOO
INFERS
IMAGINE
INTEREST

Telegrams

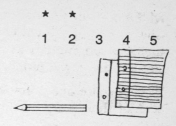

A silly but fun game, not a worthy word game.

RULES
Each player calls out several letters of the alphabet and all the players write them down as they are called. When they have a list of about ten or twelve letters, the players have five minutes to make up a telegram message. To do this they must think of a word beginning with each letter in the given order. The winner is the one to come up with the silliest telegram.

For example:

H A T I P S L W C B T M N

could become:

HELP AM TRAPPED IN POLAND STOP LOST WALLET CANNOT BEAR TO MISS NEIGHBOURS

Vowels

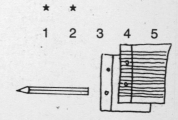

Another good vocabulary tester.

RULES
Choose one of the vowels, A, E, I, O or U. Each player then has ten minutes to come up with a list of words that contain the vowel more than once.

Players score one point every time the vowel is used in each of their words. The player with the highest score is the winner.

Here are some examples:

A   Ballad, Salad, Anagram
E   Rebel, Beetle, Feeble
I   Ripping, Civilized, Mississippi
O   Rook, Robot, Doctor
U   Sunburn, Suburb, Humdrum

Aliens

★ ★ ★ ★   ★ ★ ★
1 2 3 4 5   1   2   3   4   5

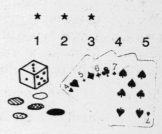

Can you rescue the sole survivor from the hordes of giant
alien monsters?

RULES

The purpose of the game is for the player (as a fearless
space-hunter) to save the abandoned ship's sole survivor
from the space creatures.

Take a pack of cards and lay them out as shown in the
diagram below, face down. The cards represent the
following:

> **Ace of diamonds** – the survivor. This is the card
> that you are looking for.
> **Jacks (any suit)** – the alien monsters. Avoid these
> at any cost. ·

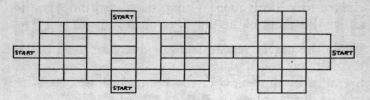

Queen of spades – the alien queen. Definitely avoid her!

Twos (any suit) – baby aliens. Nasty little things, though not as dangerous as the queen or the other aliens.

The player places the counter on the 'start', turning up this card to see what it is. If it is one of the aliens, he may fire at it; if it is neither an alien nor the survivor, he moves on, in any direction, to a next-door card which he then turns up.

The player has two main things to remember:

1 He can be 'hit' four times by the aliens before he is killed.
2 He can kill an alien by throwing a dice. He must throw a three or more to kill a baby alien, a four or more to kill a normal alien and a six to kill the alien queen.

When the player turns up a card that is an alien, he must 'fight' it, but he always gets the first chance to kill it. He throws a dice as above. If he hits the alien by throwing the right dice, then it is killed. If he fails, the alien has a go. The player must then throw the dice again to see if the alien hits him. The baby alien hits the player on the throw of a six, the normal alien on a throw of five or more and the queen on a throw of four or more. If the alien hits, the player is wounded; when he has suffered four wounds, he is dead and the game is over. If the player has not been killed then he has another

100

chance to kill the alien. This process continues until either the alien or the player is dead.

When the player reaches the survivor, he must make for the exit, taking the survivor to safety. He cannot retrace his steps by moving over the same cards he has already turned over, unless there is no choice.

HINTS
Always try to kill the alien with your first attack if you can. Remember not to go over too many cards, and to use the quickest route out when you have saved the survivor.

Boxing

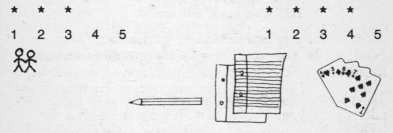

Great for playing with someone you don't like very much!

RULES
Take an ordinary pack of cards and deal them out into two hands. Draw out two 'bodies' as indicated in the diagram. Each part of the body is worth the number of points shown.

To win the game, one player must knock out the other by reducing his opponent's 'Body Points' to zero. This is done by playing the cards in a similar way to Whist

or Trumps. Each suit of cards represents a blow to a
different part of the body:

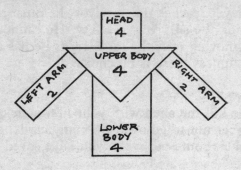

Spades   head
Hearts   upper body
Diamonds   lower body
Clubs   **even numbers,** right arm
                odd numbers, left arm

A card's value is represented by its number. (For
example, the nine of diamonds is worth nine; aces are
worth one, jacks ten, queens eleven and kings twelve.)

The players inspect their cards and then each plays one,
taking it in turns to play first. Wherever possible the
second player must play a card of the same suit as the
first (so if the first player plays a diamond, the second
player must also play a diamond if he has any in his
hand). If he cannot do this, he may play a card of his
choice but automatically loses that 'round'. The winner
is the player who has played the card with the highest
value (kings are the highest, followed by queens, then
jacks and so on down to aces which are the lowest). The
losing player deducts one point from his body.
Therefore, if a player lost a round when diamonds were
played, he would deduct one point from his 'Lower
Body'.

The used cards are put to one side. Once both players' hands have been used up, the cards are shuffled and used again. The game is won either when a player is 'knocked out' (that is, when all his points have been used up) or the cards have been used up for a second time. In this case, the winner is the one with the highest number of points left.

Whenever a player has a particular body part reduced to zero, the winner may give the loser two cards of his choice from his own hand. He then draws two of the loser's cards without looking (by doing this he can get rid of two low cards; there is no guarantee that the two cards he takes will be any higher, though).

HINTS
Although it may not at first look like it, there is scope for considerable skill in this game. Don't throw away all your high cards at the start by trying to reduce areas to zero as quickly as possible. This will allow you to get rid of your lowest cards by exchanging them with your opponent.

Cops-and-Robbers Car Chase

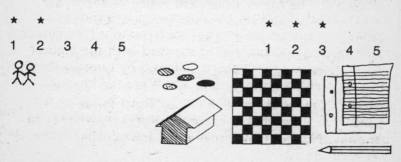

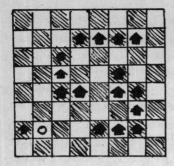
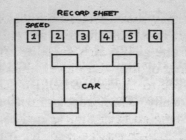

The robbers have got away. You must either stop them or smash your car to pieces trying!

RULES

Take a number of 'Monopoly'* houses or hotels and arrange them on a Draughts board to represent a small town. You may either place them as you wish or copy the set-up shown in the diagram. Then take two pieces of card or paper and draw the Record Sheets as shown. You will need them to keep track of your car's speed and damage. Take one counter to represent the Robbers and another to represent the Cops, and place them at least five squares apart on the board. Finally, decide which player will be the Cops and which the Robbers. You are now ready to play.

The Robbers move first. At the start, both cars are stationary. The player decides in which direction he wishes to move and then moves his speed marker (a counter) to the '1' position on his Record Sheet. The Cops player then does the same. On each turn, the players have a choice of either increasing or decreasing their speed by one point. The number of squares either player can move in any one turn is equal to his car's speed. The Cops should chase the Robbers, who try to get away. Neither player may use a square where a house has been placed.

Cars may move around corners by 'turning'. To turn, a player must roll the dice so that the number shown is the same as his car's speed, or more (that is, if a car has a speed of four the player must roll a four or more on the dice to 'make the bend'). Cars may not move diagonally. This process must be repeated for every right-angled turn the car makes. If a player does not score enough on the dice then his car will sustain damage equal to the number of points by which his speed exceeds the amount shown on the dice (for example, with a speed of five and a dice score of two, the car will sustain three points of damage, that is, five minus two). These are marked down on the Record Sheet.

To win, the Cops must catch the Robbers within fifteen turns. If either car has all its damage points removed (each player starts with five) the other player is automatically the winner.

HINTS
Don't be tempted to go too fast as damage points will soon add up. The Cops player should try to 'head off' the Robbers wherever possible.

*'Monopoly' is a Trademark of Waddingtons plc.

Five-A-Side Cricket

★   ★   ★   ★   ★   ★

1   2   3   4   5   1   2   3   4   5

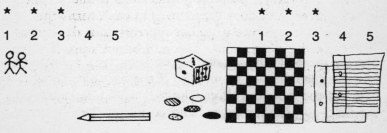

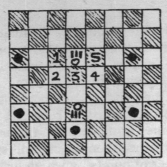

A simple sports game that can provide hours of fun.

RULES
Take five black draughts counters and place them on the board as indicated in the diagram, to represent the bowler and four fielders. Next place two coins on the board to represent the wickets. (You may if you wish draw them on pieces of card). Finally, place two white draughts as indicated, to represent the two batsmen. One player is the bowling team and the other is the batting team.

The method of play is as follows:
The bowler 'bowls' using one dice. If a one is scored, the other player, the batsman, has been bowled out. If the dice shows any other number then the batsman may hit the ball. He does this by rolling the dice twice. The first roll indicates the direction (*see* diagram). The second roll indicates how many squares the ball travels in that direction. The batsman scores one run for each square that the ball travels. Rolling a six on the first dice means that the ball has been knocked out of the ground for six runs. In this case, the batsman stays put but scores six.

Should the ball land on one of the fielders, the Batsman has been caught and is out. (So if the first dice showed a five and the second a three, the ball would be caught by the fielder in the top right-hand corner of the diagram.)

After each 'over' (six bowls), the fielding player may move one of the fielders of his choice by up to two squares.

The game continues until all five batsmen are out. The players then change sides, and the winner is the one with the highest number of runs once both sides have batted.

HINTS
Why not try a limited overs match where you only allow 50 balls to be bowled, or a proper 'Test Match' with two innings per team.

Cycle Race

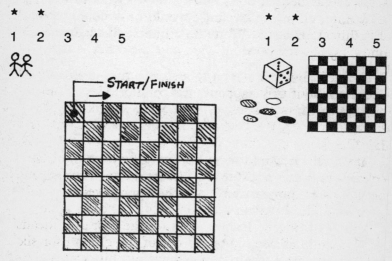

A bicycle race without the leg ache!

RULES
The game requires two sets of counters, both numbered one to four, one white and the other black. These

counters are placed on the Start Square and the two players decide which colour they want to play.

The first player rolls the two dice. He may then move his first counter either by the total of the two numbers thrown or either of the single figures. (In other words, if the six and four are thrown, he may either move his first counter four, six or ten spaces.) Having decided, he moves his first counter the correct number of spaces around the board in a clockwise direction.

The other player then does the same and moves his first counter in a similar manner. The first player then moves his number two counter and so on until all the counters have been moved. At the start of the second round, the leading counter is moved first and the others in number sequence as before. So if Black's number two counter is leading, the move sequence would be as follows: Black 2, White 1, Black 1, White 2, White 3, Black 3 and so on.

A counter cannot move on to a square that is already occupied, so if this happens, the counter does not move on that turn.

HINTS
At first sight it would seem obvious always to move a counter as far as possible. However, do not forget that one of your counters can block the opposition.

Dungeon

A sword-swishing, dragon-bashing, treasure-grabbing mega game!

RULES

The idea of the game is to explore the dungeon complex and get out alive!

First, shuffle the pack of cards and then lay the whole pack face down on the table or floor in any pattern you like. This is your dungeon complex, so make yourself some interesting winding passages with big caves to explore.

Roll two dice and add up the total. This is the number of wounds that you can suffer before being killed. Now choose any card to start the exploration of the dungeon complex. You may move your counter one card at a time, turning each up and looking at it as you progress. Most cards represent either an empty part of a cave or an empty tunnel, but some have monsters, some treasure and some both!

Nines	roll on the monster table with both dice
Tens	roll twice on the monster table with both dice

Jacks	roll on the treasure table with both dice
Queens	roll twice on the treasure table with both dice
Kings	roll on both the monster and treasure table with both dice.

MONSTER TABLE

SCORE	MONSTER	ATTACK	WOUND TOTAL
2	nothing		
3	nothing		
4	nothing		
5	GOBLIN	1 dice −2	1
6	ORC	1 dice −1	2
7	TROLL	1 dice	3
8	OGRE	1 dice +1	3
9	GIANT	1 dice +1	4
10	DEMON	1 dice +2	4
11	BLACK KNIGHT	1 dice +2	5
12	DRAGON	1 dice +3	5

The ATTACK is the number of dice the monster can throw and the + or − is the number added to the monster's dice roll (for example, if an ogre throws a four on one dice, he then adds one, making his attack total five). The player, when fighting a monster, rolls one dice. He then compares this roll with the roll of the monster. The one with the lower score is wounded and therefore loses one from his WOUND TOTAL. The player may have some bonuses to add to his score, but will have to find them first as they are magical weapons on the treasure table.

Each monster must suffer the number of wounds shown in the monster table above before it is killed.

TREASURE TABLE

SCORE	TREASURE	NOTES
2	nothing	
3	5 gold coins	
4	10 gold coins	
5	15 gold coins	
6	20 gold coins	
7	25 gold coins	
8	30 gold coins	
9	50 gold coins	
10	100 gold coins	
11	magic swords*	adds 2 to player's dice roll when attacking
12	magic shields*	reduces monster's dice roll by 2 when attacking

*A player may only have one of each. If the player already has the item then he finds 250 gold coins instead.

The player turns over the adjacent card to the one that he is on. If it is a monster, he throws on the Monster Table and he must fight whichever one he meets to the death. If it is an item of treasure, he must throw on the Treasure Table and take the loot!

The game ends if the player is killed (by losing all the wounds in his total) or if he has explored the dungeon complex totally and has survived.

HINTS
Try seeing just how much loot you can get. Keep a note of your totals and try to beat your total next time!

Escape

★ ★
1 2 3 4 5   1 2 3 4 5

An incredibly silly game for just about anywhere. One
player plays the zoo keeper and the other the escaping
animals.

RULES
To play, you will need 30 cards, ten showing a lion, ten
an elephant and ten a kangaroo. You can either draw
these up yourself or use 30 ordinary cards. (If you decide
to do this, take the ace to ten of clubs, hearts and spades
and decide which is to be which type of animal.) Now
deal the cards out into two hands.

The players then take it in turns to play a card from
their hand, but they must keep them face down and
must not look at the cards until they are played.

The idea is for the Zoo Keeper to stop the animals
escaping. Each pair of cards played has the following
results:

Elephant, Elephant ⎫
Kangaroo, Kangaroo ⎬   **Animal escapes**
Lion, Lion ⎭

Lion, Elephant ⎫
Elephant, Kangaroo ⎬   **Animal captured**
Kangaroo, Lion ⎭

112

The players keep track of how many Animals have escaped and how many have been captured. If more have escaped than have been captured, the Animal player wins. If more are captured, the Zoo Keeper wins.

HINTS
Try making the appropriate animal noises as you play the cards!

Five-A-Side Football

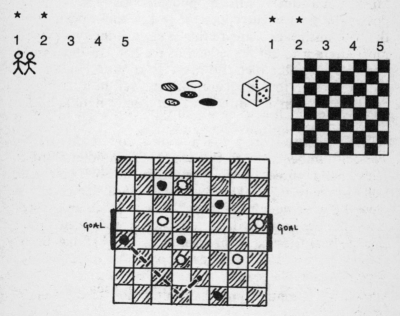

RULES
Arrange five black and five white counters on the board, as indicated in the diagram. Throw a dice to decide who gets the 'kick-off' (the higher scorer wins).

The winner places another counter to represent the ball on the same square as his goalkeeper (the counter in one of the goal squares), and throws the dice. The number shown is the distance, in squares, that the ball travels. It may move horizontally (across), vertically (up or down) or diagonally, but always in a straight line. If the ball hits the side of the pitch (the edge of the chessboard), then it will rebound back onto the pitch at a 90-degree angle.

If the ball finishes its movement on a square which has one of the kicker's own men in it, then that player may roll again and kick the ball somewhere else. If the ball finishes in a square with an opponent's piece in it, then possession goes to the opponent and he kicks next. If the ball finishes in a square that is empty, the two players must attempt to get possession of the ball. In this case, both players roll a dice and must try to move one of their pieces on to the square with the ball in it. A piece can be moved in any direction, but cannot double back on itself.

When trying to score a goal you must roll exactly the correct number to reach the goal itself. In other words, if the ball is three squares away from the goal, you must roll a three to score. The goalkeeper has a chance to save the goal though: he must throw the dice and score less than the number that the kicker scored. If he does so, the goal is saved. (For example, if the ball has been kicked three squares, the goalkeeper must roll a one or a two to save the goal.)

Play for five minutes until half time, then 'change' ends and play the second half for another five minutes. The player with the highest score is the winner.

HINTS
Try shooting at the goal when you get really close to it;

this means that the goalkeeper doesn't have much of a chance of saving it. Why not try knockout championships or make up your own league tables?

Golf

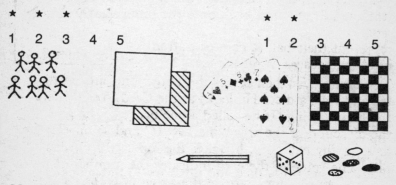

Many years ago we had a boss who loved playing golf. We invented this little game to amuse him during lunchtimes so that he wouldn't notice that we were always late!

RULES
To play you will need either a large room or, if the weather is good, the garden. Place a playing card on the ground to act as a 'tee', then place a chessboard (which represents the 'green') at least fifteen feet away from the tee. Choose one of the squares on the chessboard as the 'hole' and mark it with a coin. Take a piece of card or paper and draw up a Direction Card as shown in the diagram. Then take a pack of cards from which all the nines, tens and picture cards (that is king, queen and jack) have been removed and deal out the remaining 32 cards, face down, to the players. Finally, each player takes a different token, which can be anything, to

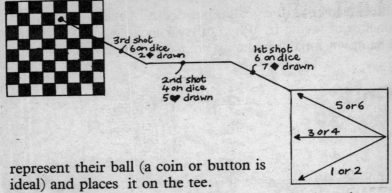

represent their ball (a coin or button is
ideal) and places it on the tee.

The first player then places the Direction Card on the
tee and rolls a dice. He looks at the Card to see where
the ball is going. If he rolled a one or a two, he goes in
the direction of the arrow marked 1/2 and so on. To see
how far the ball goes, he takes the top card from his
pile. The value of the card indicates the number of feet
the ball travels (for example the seven of clubs means
the ball travels seven feet).

The players take it in turns to hit their ball, moving in
the direction indicated by the Direction Card and the
number of feet indicated by the card they turn up each
time.

Once the ball has reached the green, the same method
is used for 'putting' except that instead of moving
distances in feet, the squares on the chessboard are used
to measure the ball's movement. Once on the green,
you do not need the exact number to get the ball into
the hole. As long as it travels over the hole, it will go in.

HINTS

Why not create your own course, either nine or eighteen
holes long, and hold your own tournament. Each hole
can be a different length, and you can if you wish invent
your own rules for bunkers and so on. Be warned! This
game can become very addictive.

Lost City

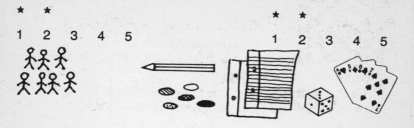

Playing the part of an intrepid Victorian explorer, can you find the Lost City before your rivals?

RULES

Take an ordinary pack of cards and remove all the kings except the king of diamonds. Then arrange the rest of the cards face down as indicated in the diagram. This represents the jungle which the players must explore. Each player then rolls a dice to decide how many explorers he has in his party and then four dice to decide how many native bearers (for example, the first roll of one dice is three, there are three explorers and if the second roll of four dice adds up to fourteen, there are fourteen bearers). Once this has been decided, each player picks a corner from which to start his exploration.

Each turn, a player may advance into any adjacent card (that is, next door), but may not move diagonally. When either player lands on a card, he should turn it face up.

Most of the cards are simply 'Jungle'. Some, however, represent hazards:

Eights (of any suit) – a trail has been found; the player may have another move.,

Nines (of any suit) – a leopard sneaks up on the party and kills an explorer.

Tens (of any suit) – you have wandered into a swamp; roll the dice and remove that number of bearers.

Jacks (of any suit) – you have been attacked by natives; lose one explorer and one dice throw's-worth of bearers.

Queens (of any suit) – you have found a clue to the whereabouts of the lost city. You may turn over one adjacent card without entering it.

Kings (of any suit) – you have found the Lost City!

The lost city contains four dice-worth of treasure (the player discovering the city rolls the dice four times and adds the results together; for example, 1/4/6/3 means that there are fourteen points of treasure in the city). Each bearer may carry one point of treasure. The winner of the game is the player to bring the most treasure back to the edge of the jungle. (For example, if a player has eight bearers, he may carry eight points of treasure.)

Should two explorers enter the same card, they may either ignore each other or fight. To fight, the players should roll one dice for every two explorers they have left and remove the number of bearers shown on the dice from their opponent. The player who loses more bearers must immediately move back to the last card he was on.

The Mile

A race game based on chance rather than skill.

RULES

Place 20 dominoes face down in a square as shown below.
Then take an ordinary pack of cards and remove all of
those with a value of eight or above (including picture
cards). Shuffle them well and then deal them out face
down to each player until all the cards are gone. Finally,
each player chooses a counter and places it on the 'Start'
domino. You are now ready to start the race.

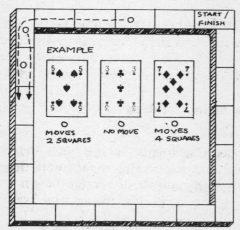

The first player draws a card from his hand and places
it face up on the table. The other players then do the
same. The values of the cards are compared and the
counters moved in the following way: the player with

119

the lowest card does not move. The other players move the number of dominoes by which their cards are higher than the lowest. (For example, as shown in the diagram, the three of hearts is the lowest and does not move. The next card, which is a five, can move two dominoes, since five is two more than three, and so on.) If the players run out of cards, they are reshuffled and dealt again. The winner is the first player to go round the track three times.

HINTS
Just learn to be lucky! If you have the right cards, you will win.

Road Race

★ ★ ★   ★ ★
1   2   3   4   5 | 1   2   3   4   5

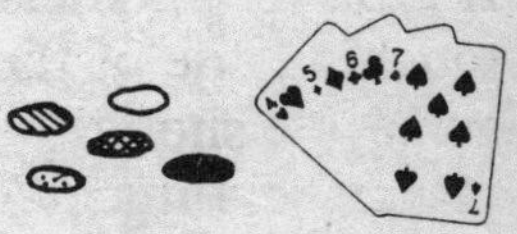

Not as tiring as the real thing.

RULES
Take two packs of ordinary playing cards, remove the nines and tens and then shuffle together the remaining cards. Place the pile face down on the floor.

Agree a Start and Finish position (both either on the floor of a large room or in the garden). The first player then takes the top card from the pack and places it face up at the start. The other player does the same. Finally, the nines and tens are scattered face down on the floor between the Start and Finish positions.

120

The first player looks at the number of the card he has put at the Start and then lays out that number of cards, face down, in a straight line towards the finish. Aces count as one and all picture cards as five. (For example, if he has a five of diamonds, he lays out five cards, as in the diagram.) The other player then does the same. On their next turn the players turn up the last card they laid out on their previous turn and advance in a similar manner.

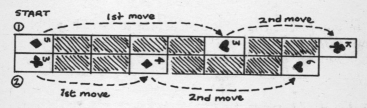

When the pack has been used up, the players should collect up all the cards except the last one in their line, reshuffle and continue play.

If a player ends his turn and the last card in his line is touching one of the cards scattered at the start of the game, he should turn it face up immediately. Should a player be unlucky and end a move with his last card touching one of the nines, he loses that turn and must move back to where he was at the end of the previous turn. If, on the other hand, he touches one of the tens he may move forward five extra car-lengths free.

The game continues until one player has reached the Finish, where he is declared the winner.

HINTS
Don't make the race too long, especially if playing with older relatives – this game can be hard on your back!

Shark

★ ★ ★ ★
1 2 3 4 5

★ ★ ★ ★
1 2 3 4 5

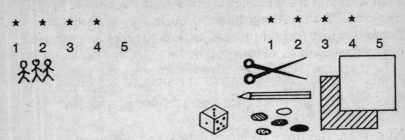

Can you rescue the swimmer before the shark gobbles him up?

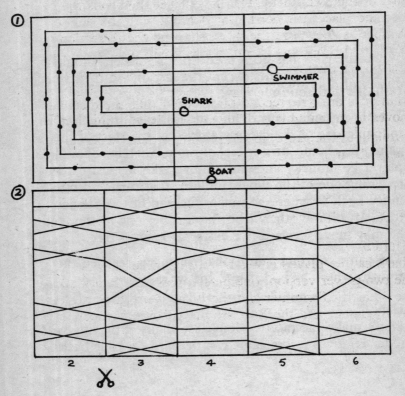

RULES

First draw up the playing boards exactly as shown in the diagram. The tracks on Board 2 must join with those on Board 1 when they are placed together. Now cut Board 2 into five sections as illustrated.

Next, make up three counters to represent the Shark, the Boat and the Swimmer. (You may use coins or some other marker if you wish.)

Now place the three counters as marked on Board 1. You are now ready to play.

Each player decides who they want to be (the Shark, the Boat or the Swimmer). The first player then rolls the dice and places the portion of Board 2 with the same number as shown on the dice on to the centre section of Board 1. (If a one is rolled, use Board 1 as it is.) The first player then rolls the dice again and may move the number of dots shown by the dice along the line his counter is on. The second player then rolls the dice and moves in the same way. This method is continued throughout the game, in the playing order: Swimmer, Shark, Boat.

The Shark wins if he manages to land exactly on the Swimmer. If the Swimmer reaches the Boat before this happens, these two players win.

HINTS

Shark can be played either by two or three players. In the two-player version, one person plays the Shark and the other the Swimmer and the Boat. With three players, the Swimmer and the Boat are played by different players who must work as a team.

Stock Exchange

★ ★ ★ ★

★ ★ ★ ★

1 2 3 4 5

1 2 3 4 5

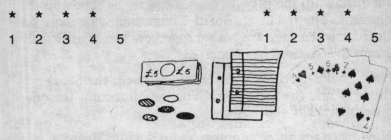

All the thrills of the Stock Exchange for the price of a pack of cards.

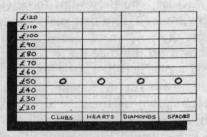

	CLUBS	HEARTS	DIAMONDS	SPADES
£120				
£110				
£100				
£90				
£80				
£70				
£60				
£50	O	O	O	O
£40				
£30				
£20				

RULES

Take a pack of cards and remove all the picture cards (the kings, queens and jacks). Shuffle these and leave them in a pile face down on the table. Sort out the rest of the pack into their suits (clubs, diamonds, spades and hearts) and then place them face up in four piles. These are called the stock exchange.

Draw up the record sheet as shown in the diagram and place one counter for each company on the £50 squares. Finally, give each player £500 of 'Monopoly'* money, placing the rest to one side. This is called the bank. One of the players is now chosen to look after this money and is called the banker.

The aim of this game is to buy and sell shares on the

'stock exchange'. The winner is the first player to own 30 shares in two different companies.

The four different suits represent shares in the following companies:

Clubs	health clubs
Hearts	private hospitals
Diamonds	mines
Spades	building firms

Each 'pip' on a card represents one share in a company, (for example the seven of hearts represents seven shares in private hospitals, an ace of clubs would be a single share in a health club and so on).

The price of a single share (or 'pip') is shown on the record sheet (at the start of the game all shares cost £50 each).

In a turn, a player may decide either to buy *or* sell shares; *he may not do both*. To buy shares, the player looks through the relevant pile of cards in the stock exchange and picks out the ones he wants to buy (for example, if he wanted to buy nine shares in private hospitals he could simply take the nine of hearts from the pile; he could, if he wished, take the four and five instead, or any other combination adding up to the correct amount). A player may buy as many shares as he wishes (and can afford!) in his turn and is not limited to one company. Once he has taken the shares he needs he pays for them (the number of shares he has bought multiplied by the current price) and pays it to the bank. He removes the shares (cards) that he has just bought from the stock exchange and places them in front of him.

Selling shares follows the same method, although this time cards are taken from the owning player and placed back in the stock exchange. After working out the price, the player then takes that amount from the bank and keeps it.

Just as on the real stock exchange, the prices in this game can go up and down. Every time someone buys shares in a company, a note is made and the price moved one 'notch' up at the end of his turn. If shares are sold then the same method is used but the price is moved one 'notch' down. (For example, if a player bought shares in private hospitals during his turn at a cost of £50 per share, then the price would be changed to £60 at the end of his turn.)

After every player has had a turn, one of the face-down picture cards is turned face up. These have the following effects:

Jack the value of shares in the jack's suit are reduced by £30.

Queen no trading is allowed in shares of the queen's suit during the next round of turns.

King the value of shares in the king's suit is increased by £30.

(For example, if a queen of spades is turned up then no one can buy or sell shares in building firms during the next round. If a king of diamonds is turned up, £30 is immediately added to the cost of shares in mines.)

The game ends when one player has gained control of 30 shares in two different companies.

HINTS

Try buying up the lower cards first. This will force the other players to spend more, since all the lower cards will be gone.

In the latter stages of the game be careful of what you sell. Other players may be waiting for a certain card in order to win the game.

Each player should keep the cards he has bought hidden from the others.

*'Monopoly' is a trademark of Waddingtons Games Ltd.

Treasure Vault

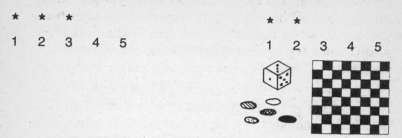

The perfect game for any budding 'Indiana Jones'!

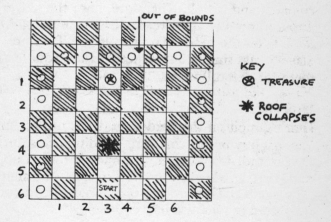

RULES
Take a draughts board (to represent the Treasure Vault) and place the men (counters) as shown in the diagram. Then place a coin to represent the 'Treasure' and a chessman to represent the 'Adventurer' in the square marked 'Start'. The Adventurer must reach the Treasure and then return to the start with it. He may move one square per turn in any direction.

Now this all sounds very easy until you realize that the Vault is crumbling round you! Each turn roll two dice.

127

These are used to decide where the roof collapses during that turn. Read the first dice against the vertical scale (up the side of the board) and the second against the horizontal (along the bottom). A roll of four and three would cause the roof to collapse as indicated on the diagram.

Squares where the roof has collapsed block the Adventurer's path and he must move round them. If he is unlucky enough to be hit on the head, he must return to the beginning and start again. The roof can never collapse on the Treasure itself; if this does happen, just ignore it and re-roll. Therefore, once the player is actually carrying the Treasure, he is immune from 'bumps on the head'. To pick up the Treasure, the player must simply enter the Treasure square and stay there for one full turn.

HINTS
Don't get hit on the head!